I0160021

# DRAGON EYES

Edmonton Garrison, Edmonton Alberta Canada    2011

ISBN# 97-0-9813261-8-4
Copyright © 1st 5th 2011

Dedicated to my dear friend Brian Metcalfe
& in loving memory of Adeline Pearson

www.nuts4mars.com

Billy Bobs (Thornton message)   -   HEART shaped jet trails

Calgary Trail south, 60 Ave. Edmonton  -    Cdn CF-18 Hornets

PHANTOM OPS

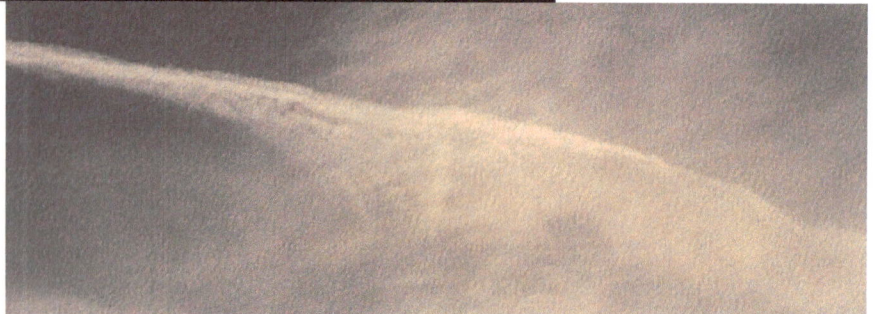

## OPEN STARGATE / Q5 LEAP is a Phantom Ops & assists as Special Reconnaissance

## To the Knights of Mars being the Military/coalition, Law, Spyland, & Select Viewers

1st 5th works as a trained Psychic volunteer assist for Special Reconnaissance. 1st 5th's daily Remote Viewed Psi painting & script is accessed by Security. Q5 Leap is hopeful that in timely fashion this will extend to include the wounded warriors. This trail requires commitment, Psychic development and faith. Rewarding it's followers with fascinating, adventuresome discovery on a current, unfolding Star Trail. MILITARY - Canadian (Edmonton Garrison, local), US, UK, (with English Royals). with Coalition members (some security for Pope Benedict XVI); LAW enforcement -Fusion Centers, FBI, RCMP, Spyland etc; and on an MI:8 basis, the occasional Search & Rescue ie: if you fall off a Cruise Ship or get lost on top of a Mountain, they will call in the experienced Psychic to provide an *extra* assist. 1st 5th was initially used on Mars Reconnaissance raw footage -NASA Rovers Opportunity & Spirit.

### PHANTOM OPS - 1st 5th & Q5 Leap Psi - Knights of Mars Star Trail Talent

| | | |
|---|---|---|
| Tom Cruise | Ca Gov Arnold Schwarzenegger | Jackie Chan |
| Sylvester Stallone | Bruce Willis | Clint Eastwood |
| Kurt Russell | Kevin Costner | John Hannah |
| Owen Wilson | Eddie Murphy | Brendan Fraser |
| Vin Diesel | Harrison Ford | Gary Sinise |
| Paul Hogan | Nicolas Cage | John Travolta |
| Christian Slater | Richard Dean Anderson | George Clooney |
| Billy Bob Thornton | Mel Gibson | Will Smith |
| Dan Akroyd | Danny Glover | Tommy Lee Jones |
| Richard Dreyfuss | Johnny Depp | Kiefer Sutherland |
| Antonio Banderas | Charlton Heston | Steve McQueen |
| William Shatner | Viggo Mortensen | Chuck Norris |
| Leonard Nimoy | Martin/Charlie/Emilio Sheens | Keanu Reeves |
| Steven Seagal | Mel Gibson | Jason Statham |
| Jet Li | Sean Connery | Kevin Bacon |
| Ben Stiller | Jon Voight | Robert De Niro |
| Wesley Snipes | Thomas Jane | Karen Allen |
| Angelina Jolie | Brad Pitt | Jeff Bridges |
| Snoop Dogg | Eric Roberts | Tony Cox |

**Expendables** starring Sylvester Stallone & Jason Statham

**XM25 SUPERGUN & GRENADE LAUNCHER currently in Afghanistan; happy emote**

Edmonton Alberta, Canada     CF-18 Hornets Sky Show

WAR SHIP USS GEORGE WASHINGTON  with South Korea for War Games Dec 2010

US  Japan  -War Games Dec 2010

Operation Keen Sword

Troops on the ground Afghanistan 2010

QATAR Jet - coalition forces in Libya 2011

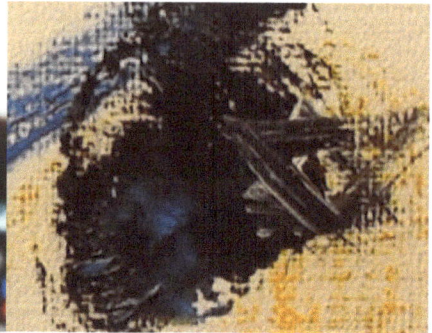

Officer of the Law, emote ; Akron, Ohio Bad guys; teens on a rampage;

(below) Perfect Storm starring George Clooney;  Edm Ab CF-18 Sky Trails

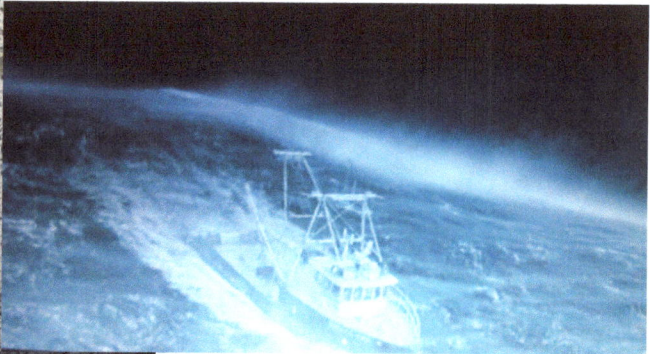

Heisenberg proved that at subatomic levels we experience what we classify as Quantum Mechanics. Since then, our reality substance has been shown to be operating at levels of the 5th Dimension, inclusive of the 4th. Furthermore, Open Stargate has the phenomenon pegged as being composed of both Space Light & Time Light elements, being part of Space TimeLight.

Planet Earth with Water World/Navy theme imagery; google earth type remote viewed psychic discipline painting; ark shape of emotes meaning Ship; (above, far right) US Chairman of the Joint Chiefs of Staff, Adm Mike Mullen's emote form, note the whale and flipper's fluked edging on it's form as well as the Navy explicits.

Samurai swords (sideways)  US & Japan War Games Operation Keen Sword

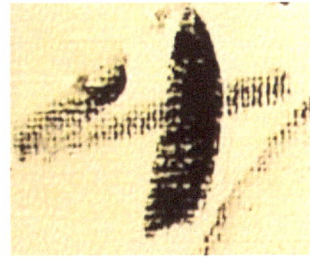

Top kick emote; match to satellite deployment psi paints below

2006 Pegasus ; Military probe returned successfully to Earth; sky trails

## Isaiah

Chapter 43 Verse 15-20

":15 I *am* the LORD, your Holy One, the creator of Israel, your King.

:16 Thus saith the LORD, which maketh a way in the sea, and a path in the mighty waters:

:17 Which bringeth forth the chariot and horse, the army and the power; they shall lie down together, they shall not rise: they are extinct, they are quenched as tow.

:18 Remember ye not the former things, neither consider the things of old.

19. Behold, I will do a new thing; now it shall spring forth; shall ye not know it? I will even make a way in the wilderness, *and* rivers in the desert.

:20 The beast of the field shall honour me, **the dragons and the owls;** because I give waters in the wilderness *and* rivers in the desert, to give drink to my people, my chosen. "

Open Stargate/Q5 Leap/Phantom Ops emotes

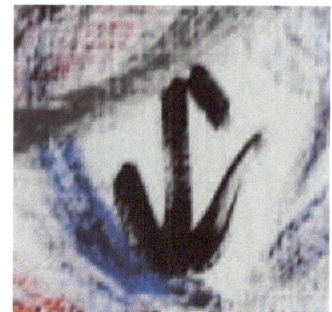

original 'Stargate' - Info Swann emote

Surprise visit to Afghanistan Dec 6th, 2010 US Defence Secretary Robert Gates

US Secretary of Defence, Robert Gates, RV with emote, Pterodactyl beak,
Bottom of the form in rust tones, near the center.

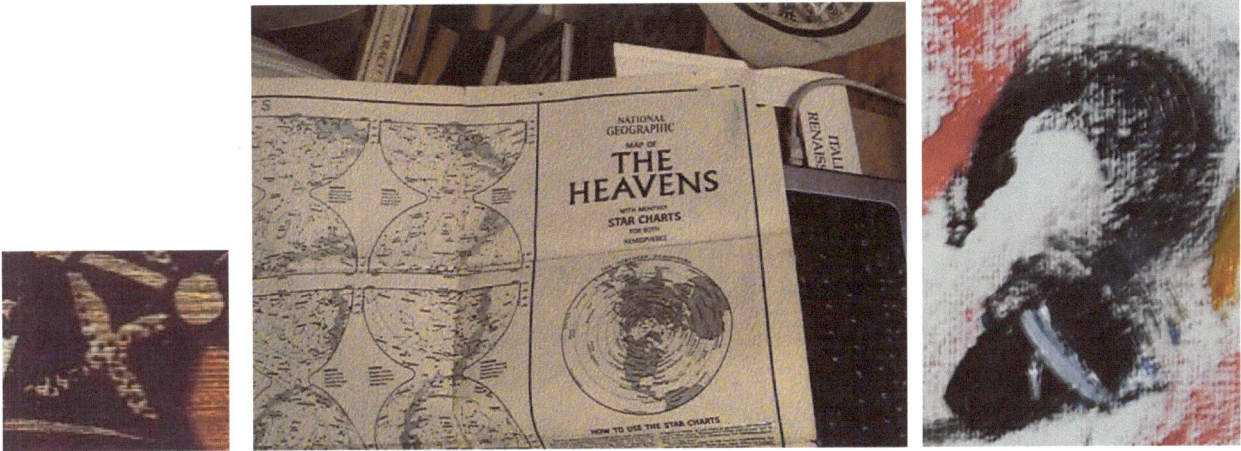

As in, Oh the Star Maps are 'the Star Maps' ...wow for one; it's Quantum Psi reality structuring; distinct patterning of the 'egg timer' shape to the celestial sphere maps; and on the end at far right, above, is the Dragon form Emote for Phantom Ops, Dec 7th, 2010

PHANTOM OPS    Special Reconnaissance

Brilliant Girl   pen & ink;  JETS Sky Trails -  Edmonton Alberta CANADA Dec 9th, 2010

Phantom Ops Psi emotes for Star Trail discoverers

perhaps future Psi warriors for certain wounded warriors

EXPENDABLES     starring  Sylvester Stallone & Jason Statham

Psi paint of Sylvester Stallone in Expendables

KNIGHT & DAY starring Tom Cruise; on the railing

Dragon & Owls - Tom Cruise emote; Cruise drive by of Q5 Leap s 1st 5th

KNIGHT AND DAY starring Tom Cruise - rolling vehicle; touch down RV

## Gideon's Bible Isaiah Chapter 43

: 8 Bring forth the blind people that have eyes, and the deaf that have ears.

:9  Let all the nations be gathered together, and let the people be assembled: who among them can declare this, and shew us former things? Let them bring forth their witnesses, that they may be justified: or let them hear, and say, It is truth.

:10 Ye are my witnesses, saith the LORD, and my servant whom I have chosen: that ye may know and believe me, and understand that I am he; before me there was no God formed, neither shall there be after me.

11. I, even I, am the LORD and beside me there is no saviour.

12. I have declared, and have saved and I have shewed, when there was no strange god among you; there fore ye are my witnesses, saith the LORD, that I am God." ...

**:15 I am the LORD, your Holy One, the creator of Israel, your King.**

:16 Thus saith the LORD, which maketh a way in the sea, and a path in the mighty waters;

"17 Which bringeth forth the chariot and horse, the army and the power, they shall lie down together, they shall not rise: they are extinct they are quenched as tow,

"18 Remember ye not the former things, neither consider the things of old.

"19 Behold, I will do a new thing; now it shall spring forth; shall ye not know it? I will even make a way in the wilderness, and rivers in the desert.

:20 The beast of the field shall honour me, **the dragons and the owls; because I give waters in the wilderness, and rivers in the desert to give drink to my people the chosen.**

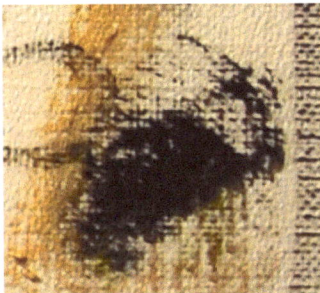
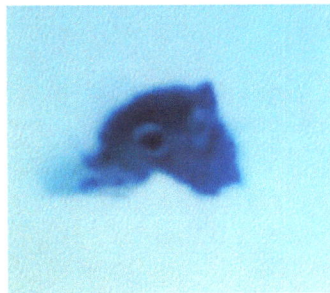

Squirrel in the snow

Shields Q5 Leap Britain, Dec 2010 youth riots

ISAF

## Russian missiles

Troops in Afghanistan 2010

South Korea - tanks; silver & gold

Phantom Ops emote;  Edmonton AB sky;  NY Cops - (bomb scare)  *it was nothing*

*Pentagon Vice Admiral William E. Gortney*

*Pentagon Col Lapan*

*Mc Knight had to eat bugs to survive shot down behind enemy lines; USS Kearsarge rescue*

Bannerman Castle, New York (USA) above West Point

Troops

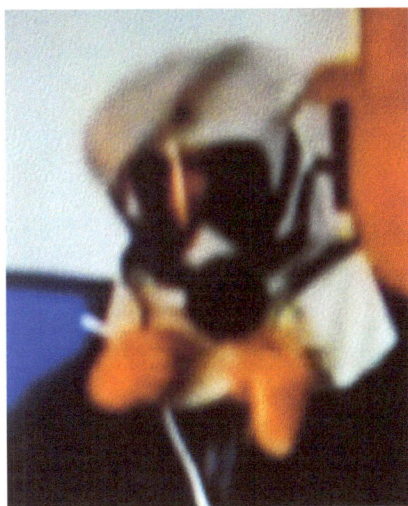

S Korea tests, Dec 2010; gas mask and RV

Emote form linked to the troops leaving Iraq, this time the emote form has boots on -
USS Harry Truman returned successfully; the requisite boots tossed off the end
Signalling no loss of life on the mission...

September 9th, 2001 Responders - Firemen

M1 Tanks     Afghanistan Dec 2010

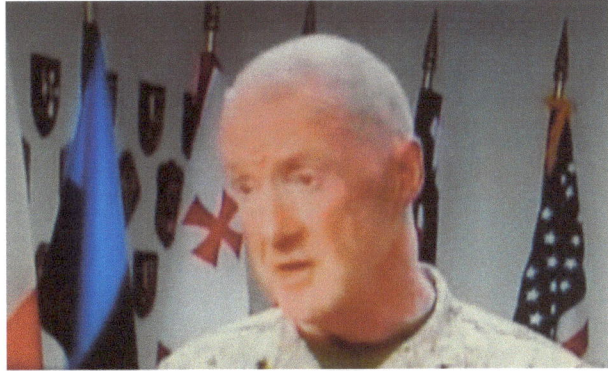

US Marine Commandant Gen Amos; Maj Gen Richard Mills     Afghanistan Christmas 2010

Sky Trails  Edmonton, Alberta; Israeli Red Team training Jets emote

NEW YEARS EVE Times Square New York NY

Phantom Ops appearance - Owen Wilson -

Owen Wilson Star talent at Times Square (NY) New Year s bash 2011

Mayor Bloomberg, NY, (left) with Medal of Honour recipient, Staff Sgt Sal Giunta, dropping the Crystal Ball at New Year's Eve festivities, Times Square, NY 2011

David Garret talented violinist (World's fastest)

Marine at Times Square, to be made a Major on Jan 1st, 2011; Psi paint of his cap

I pulled up Matrix starring Keanu Reeves in precog Oracle fashion the day before there was an incident where hundreds of rounds of ammunition were set off in a suitcase, by a primer accident, USA, Miami, Dec 29th, 2010. Matching bullets in Psi paint.

## South Korea warriors 2011

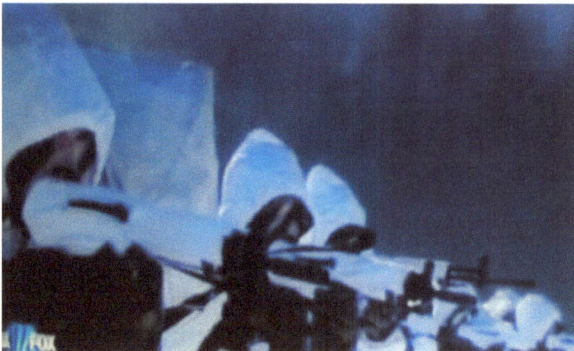

South Korea

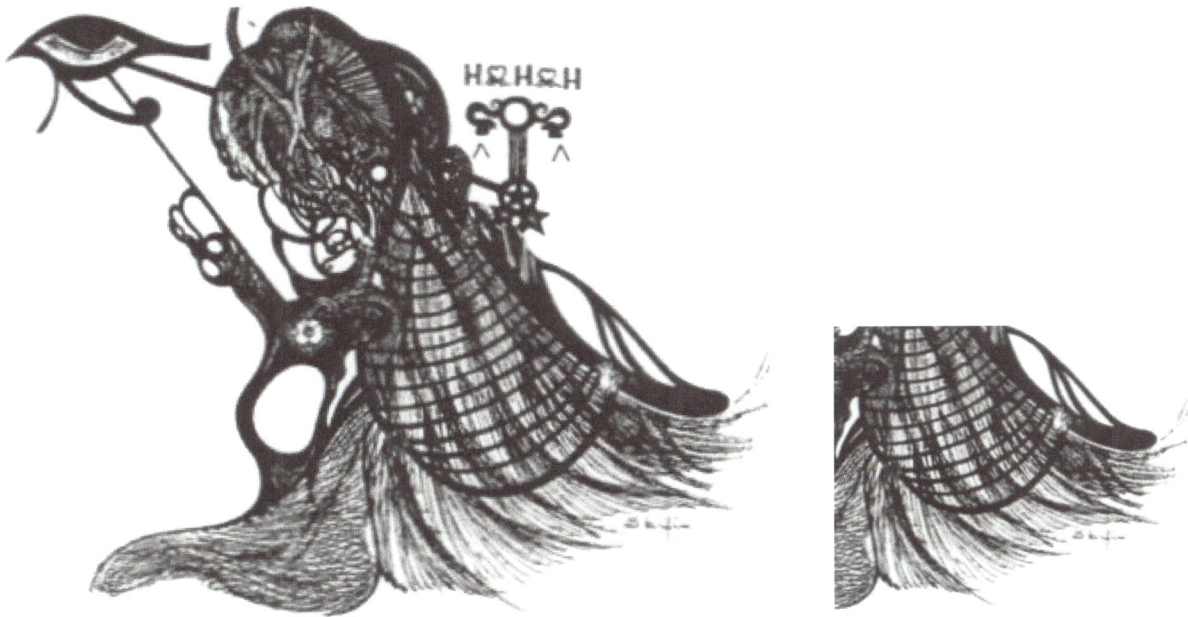

South Korean brush for trail cover; match to the older Remote Viewed pen&ink by 1ˢᵗ 5ᵗʰ

Flight craft

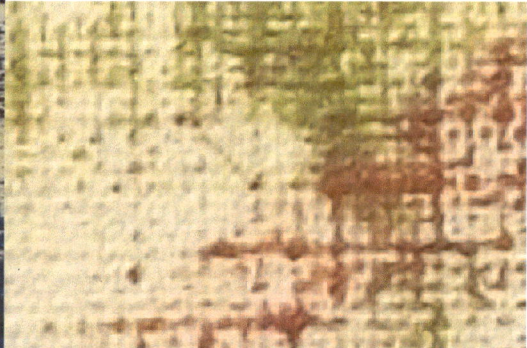

South Korean choppers revolving tails in unison

British Bobbies hat

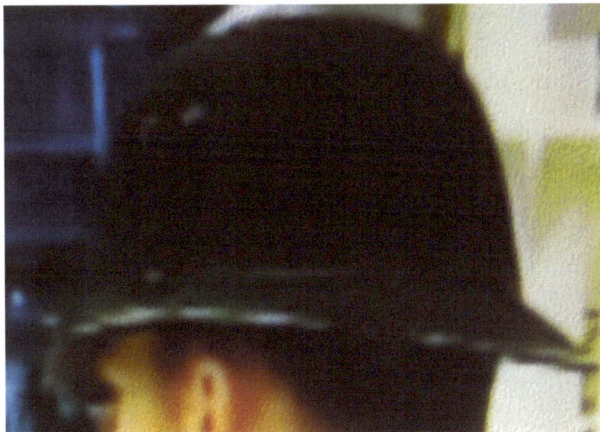

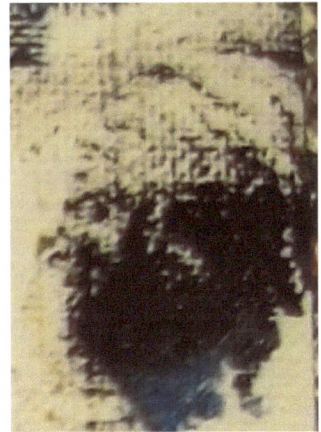

44 Magnum (diagonal); match to gun in  Dirty Harry starring Clint Eastwood

FBI Chief  Robert Mueller III Remote View, Jan 9th/2011

Edm AB sky trails

New York, NY (USA) Police Commissioner Ray Kelly and Rep Peter King (NY-R)

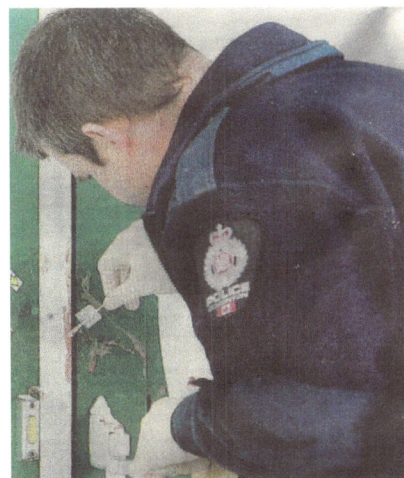

Edmonton Police gathering blood evidence  Jan 9th

Queensland, Australia - January 2011 major flooding and inland tsunami

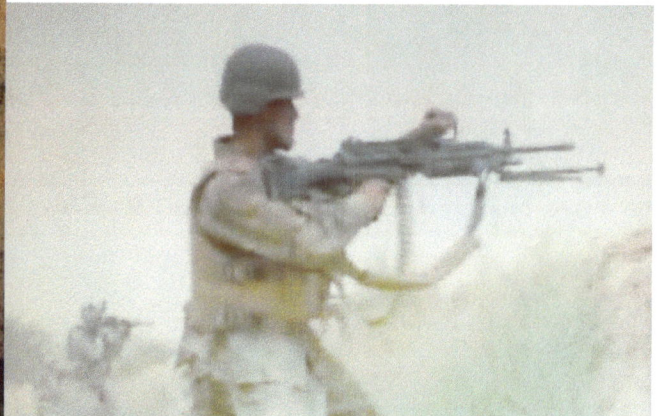

Large Gun - troops in Afghan, Jan 2011 - The American  starring George Clooney

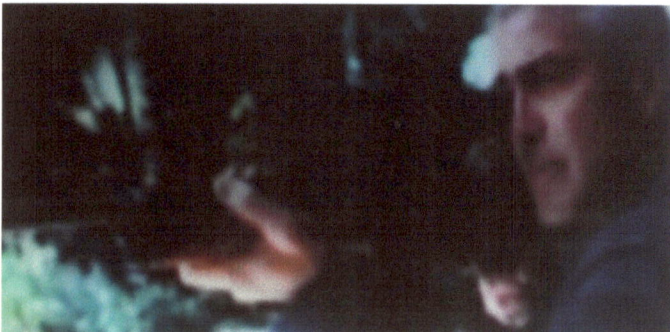

Star Trek  starring William Shatner & Leonard Nimoy

Knights Visor - George Clooney with emote sword/sand horizon

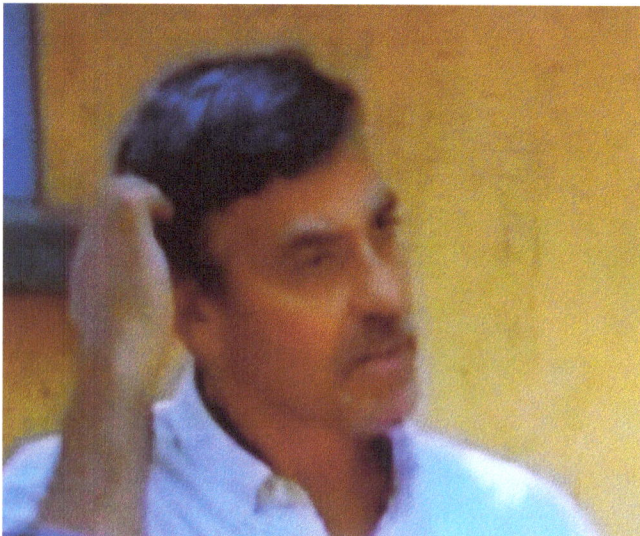

Scratching his head, a match to the Remote View psi paint (above, left)

Sky Trails Edmonton, Alberta, Canada

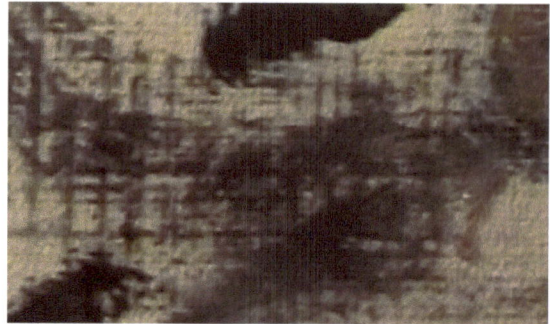

Afghan trained soldier's helmet Remote View Jan 2011

Soldiers Jan 11, 2011 Afghanistan; seated in circles

Catastrophic flooding Queensland, Australia -rains November 2010 to January 2011

Aussie flood 2011 man on board

De Havilland *Mosquito*

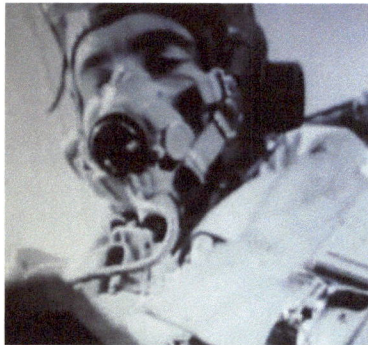

RV empathic emote psi trained code; De Haviilland DHC-4 Caribou; C-130 air craft

Watch the psychic/pixel match pc release by 1st 5th video clip up at
You Tube -Psychic Trained by Military New Zealand - de Havilland DHC-4 Caribou
http://www.youtube.com/watch?v=kjrRhg-_Lxw

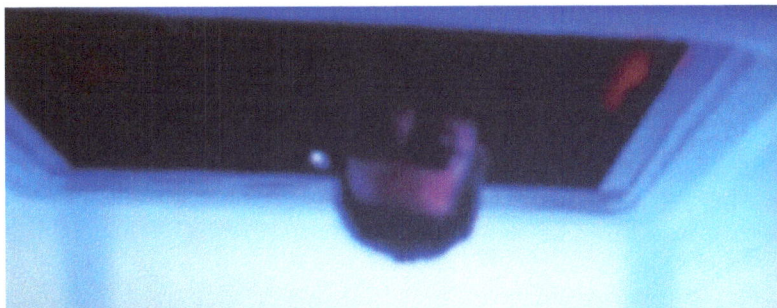

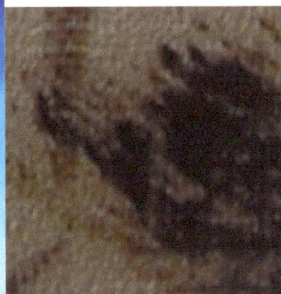

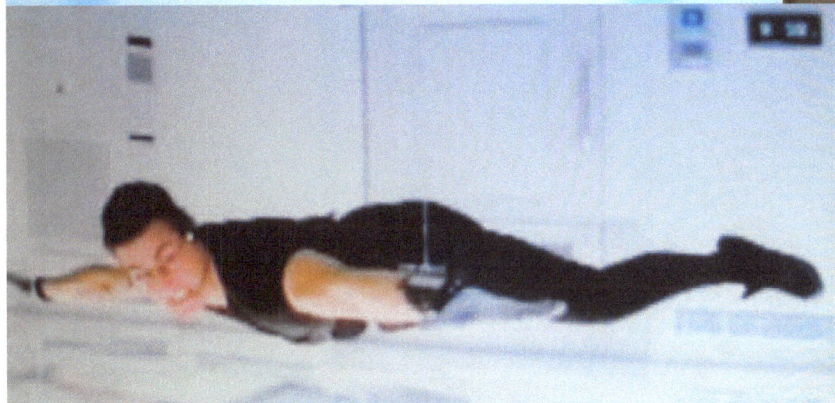

MISSION IMPOSSIBLE ONE    starring  TOM CRUISE

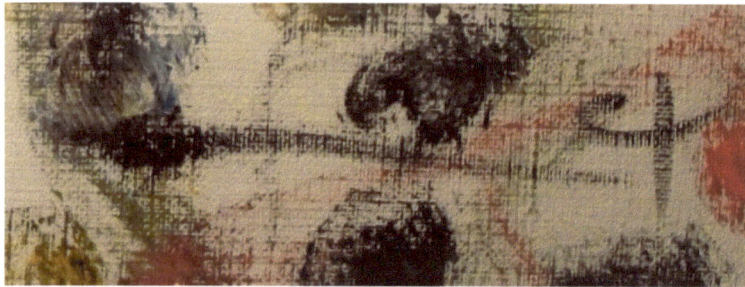

Jon Voight , MI: One

Conor Powell, correspondent in Afghanistan; window form RV pattern recognition marker

Military females in Combat 2011

Galvanized metal culvert - troops in Afghanistan 2011

**Chinese Martial Arts Swords**

Chinese Martial Arts Swords

**The General and the Gentleman**

MARTIAL ARTS OUTPOST

**The General AKA. The Chinese Dao**

Chinese Sabre - MARTIAL ARTS  Jan 19 2011  Sword & emotes

Blade's edge on horizontal

Shanghai Knights visual visor marker and visual for a Sand Eel or Chan Launce (right)

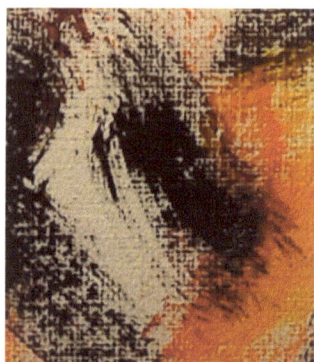

Sabre and emote at far right visually describing a 'dancing sword'; AB sky trails

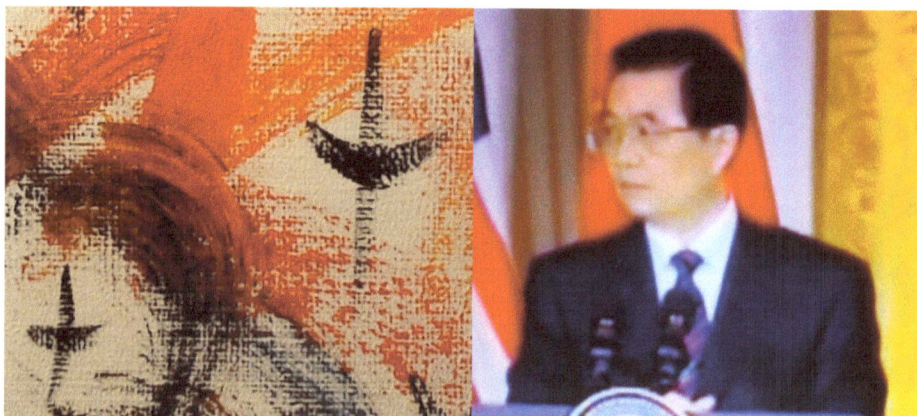

President of China Hu Jintao RV visiting the WH in the USA Jan 2011

US Sec of Defence Robert Gates at the Great Wall of China, Jan 2011

## Brad Pitt & Angelina Jolie  -  engagement  Jan 2011

Jolie & Pitt emotes

## special  Wing Sky by Canadian CF-18 Hornets jets/Q5 Leap Sun Fire Ops

# George Clooney & Angelina Jolie in DARFUR

Angelina Jolie

Camp for Darfur refugees

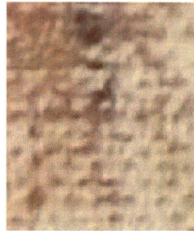

George Clooney, also in Darfur

or Darfur refugees

Darfur, Sudan, Africa   2011

USA WEST POINT – 444 Iran Hostages, 1 former Marine, reunite 30 years later

China / Martial Arts - emote     Tiger Remote View psi paint     Dinosaur close up

Original Psi paint of my pal's Dinosaur bone from Drum Heller , Alberta, Canada  (upper right)

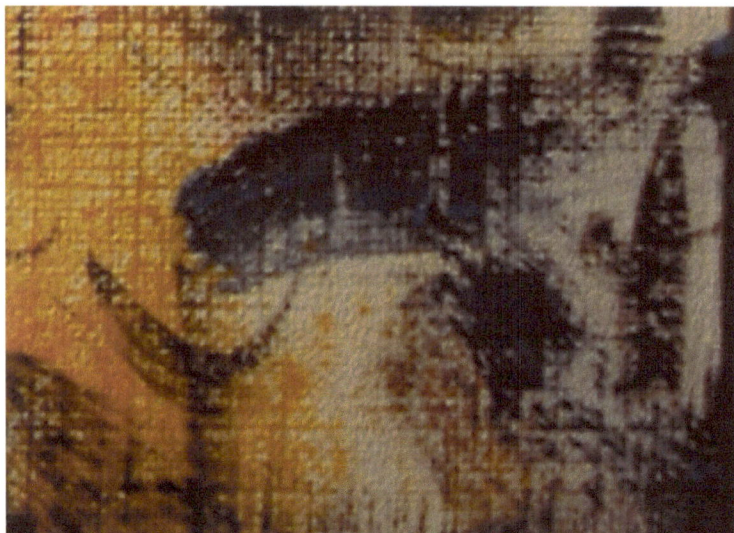

*Royal Canadian Parliament/Crown marker and visuals Jan 28/ 2011*
*I heard that …. 'Lucky they don't have you in a bloody kennel' ….*
*;complete knife RV psi paint and what appears to be an Oriental mask*

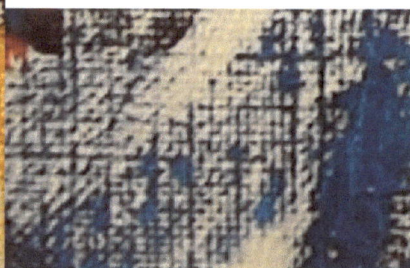

*Blue small visuals of air craft in this context Military; If you get the angle right there is a great Yoda tracing, with the ear tips*

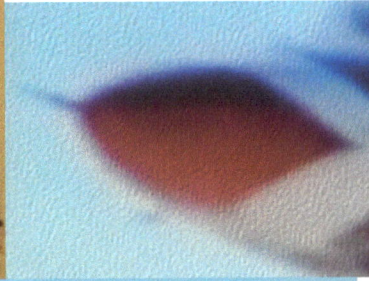

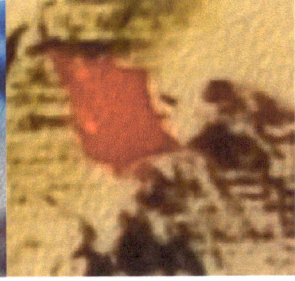

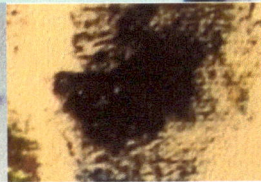

Nellis AFB Nevada, USA

**XM25 Laser Rifle**

Binoculars

12 Monkeys starring Bruce Willis;  Long Guns

Abydos, Egypt ancient hieroglyphs, modern times link;
see 'Ancient Links & Future Trails' by 1ˢᵗ 5ᵗʰ at Amazon.com for more on the *Star Trail - Chariot Papyrus*

RV painted psi visuals often skip along. As shown by this hieroglyph set. The tail slant of the modern day chopper matches to the far right top corner of the 'glyph (above left Abydos tablet), at the far under side of the tank form, albeit upside down/reversed. There is a visual match between the wide angled lines of the chopper and the tablet corner tank. RV is decoded and linked up dot2dot For matching colors, shapes, meanings; message encapsulations we attempt to connect/read as they link into our times' security concerns. An ongoing process, Remote Viewing can be a streaming running script as well as the Psi paints of trained code.

According to the Archaeo-astronomer JAWs John Anthony West, author of the book "Serpent in the Sky: High Wisdom of Ancient Egypt" who has been to the Abydos actual carvings, this set that matches out modern times Military's equipment, is regarded by conventional wisdom as a mere ***palimpsest*** - two different times of carving one over the over. That's his understanding. However, that is not the current knowledge if you are a trained by the Military and with many years of experience Remote Viewer using the illusive but substantial Quantum 5ᵗʰ D as a window to elsewhere/when (an ability of the Quantum reality structure, that has been amply confirmed and studied is the reversed arrow of time; see HALDRON etc).

I have even managed while working, to moonlight a book 'Ancient Links & Future Trails' available at Amazon on the matter of the clear and time synched in material in ancient Egyptian hieroglyphs. The unusual factoid is, we work the codes and trained Viewing daily, all day every day, and often into the night, and there may at times be found that very oddity, the superimposed imagery and overlapping theme content in a singly proportioned Quantum encapsulation. In other words, that's normal, it happens, in Remote Viewing where the psychic phenomenon links up in that fashion. Which is not to imply that's the only way, not at all. But if there was some additional timed reason for the RV Descriptive, again another term that comes into play only this one 'descriptive' more often, that there was an extra layer, or double rendition or other effect that being shown to us. We have to read the messages in the visual (and written RV) content. And you have to know the language of it, just like any other to read it. The Remote Viewer 1ˢᵗ 5ᵗʰ studied for years, trained Psychic by the Military; and we use computers with visual pixel match release. It's not speculation, it's confirmed visual matches. Like the ancient hieroglyphs of Egypt, the RV also has different components, the visual and the phonetic. The audio/visual distinctions and overlap, descriptive as well as the precision material we glimpse when Viewing.

A startling conclusion is they had masterful Viewers with far less clutter around them, more finely tuned senses and some not all but some of the ancient material is linking in terms of time synch and Quantum 5ᵗʰ D Leap. They had Remote Viewers, as the artists/scribes who left a trail for a Master Viewer such as 1ˢᵗ 5ᵗʰ to find, surface, link to and decode. I have used the Chariot papyrus for some time now, with truly amazing visual links between it's time and ours. In fact it is certain, not speculation, that ancient Egypt had Master Remote Viewers, whether you call the psi talent's skill set Oracle or Prophecy.

Precision matched to RV of Chariot Papyrus; matching gun visuals

(Fmr) Pres Ronald Reagan on 100ᵗʰ Birthday celebration. Reagan was a key player in the former Remote Viewing developments, operating out of Ft. Bragg (USA)

RV Titanic, black for deep water no light, descriptive ; Shovel (crime tip/clue)

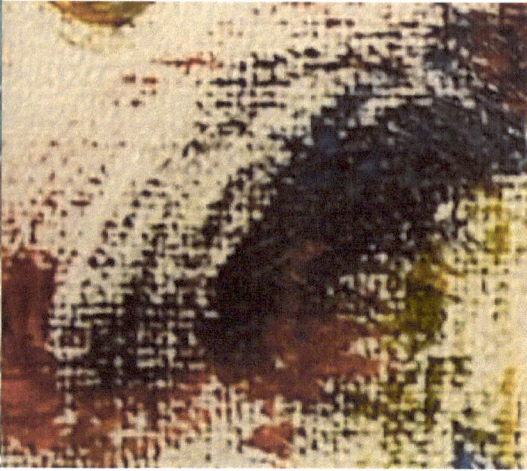

**Psi Paint by 1st 5th;** Troops small, helmets; Egyptian Revolt 2011  Military tanks

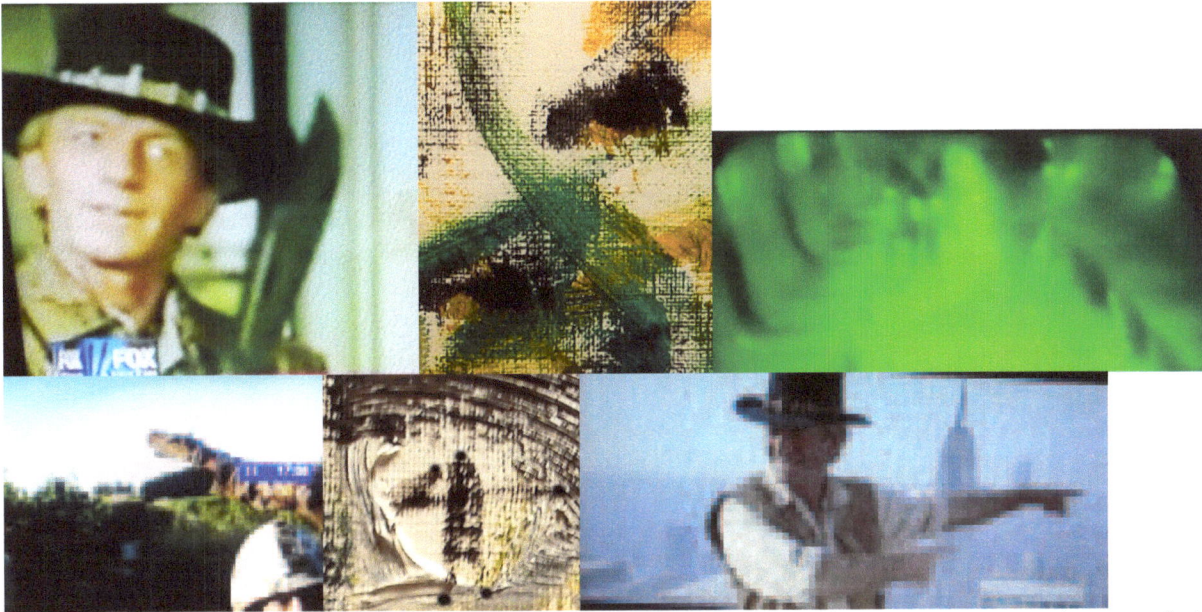

*Crocodile Dundee starring Paul Hogan* -green Knife/ troops night green eyes match to small alien atop heap on back cover of Dragon Eyes; Canadian Troops pointing in Afghanistan, with emote

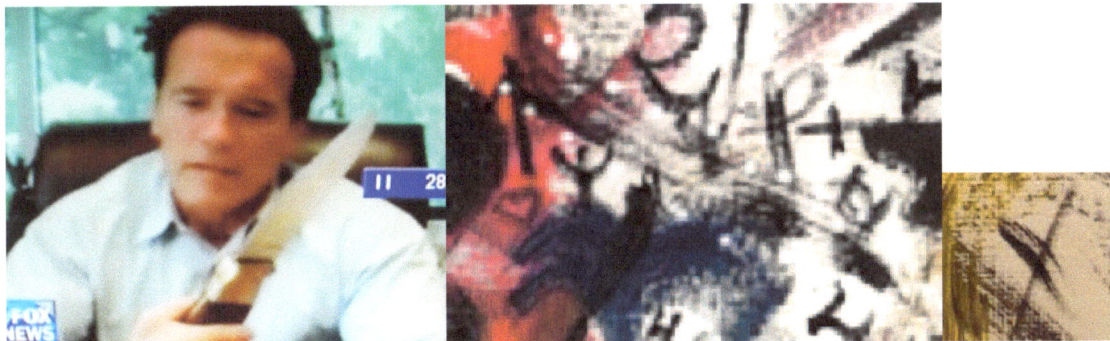

(Fmr) Gov Arnold Schwarzenegger with Commando Knife match to RIP RV knife

Punisher starring John Travolta & Thomas Janel John Travolta - Pilot endorsement, 40 years of Flight

Rolls Royce PHANTOM - British Royal wedding car Prince William & Kate Middleton

Rolls Royce Phantom RV psi paint

Royal Wedding with tiara and official Witch emote

## Blade starring Wesley Snipes - Vampires & Garlic

# French - Libya no fly zone 1st strike - 4 of Gaddafi's tanks

*USS Stout & USS Whitney - Libya no fly zone- TOMAHAWK CRUISE MISSILES*

*Army General Carter Ham*

1   British submarine Remote View psi painting; fired missiles at Col Gaddafi's compound, Libya

2   Dark shadowed side of the pyramid and matching dark tall triangle RV
Psi by 1st 5th just before Tunisia/Egyptian Revolution 2011

3   Afghan Military training by NATO 2011 with gun RV

4   Open Stargate assist with pipe suggestion amid nuclear meltdown fears Fukushima, Japan .

CANADIAN FIGHTER JET - Libya no fly zone 2011

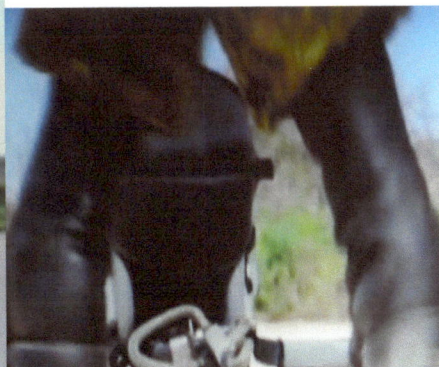

Edmonton, Alberta  Sky Trails

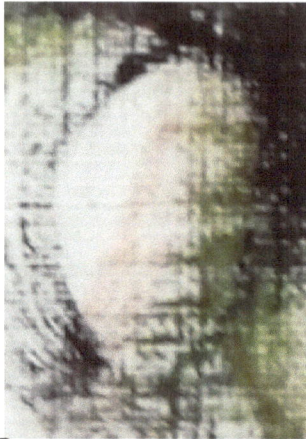

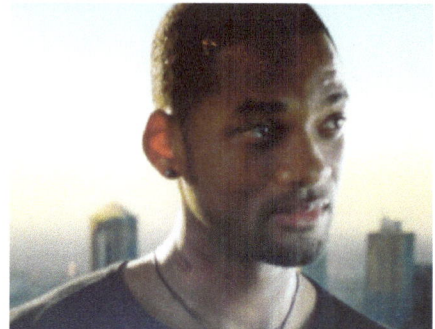

*I ROBOT  starring  Will Smith*

El Sereno, CA

HOT

*Gaggle of Cops remember, they're everywhere*

Libya  no fly zone  British Jet refuelling

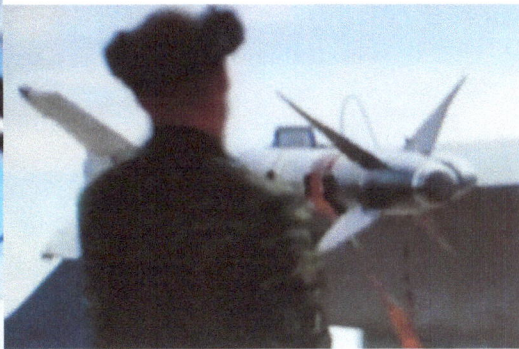

Canadian jets Libya  Operation Odyssey Dawn 2011

match to Quantum Psi Painting by 1ˢᵗ 5ᵗʰ top left striking blue

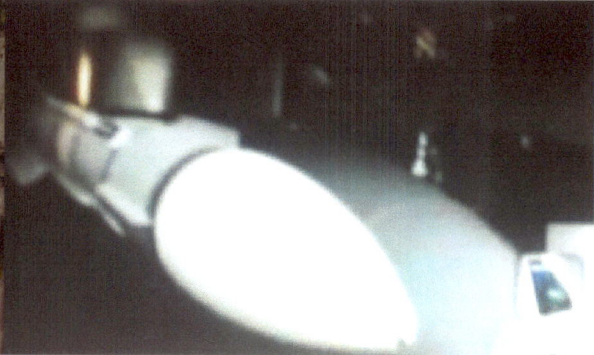

USA Fighter Jet Pilots

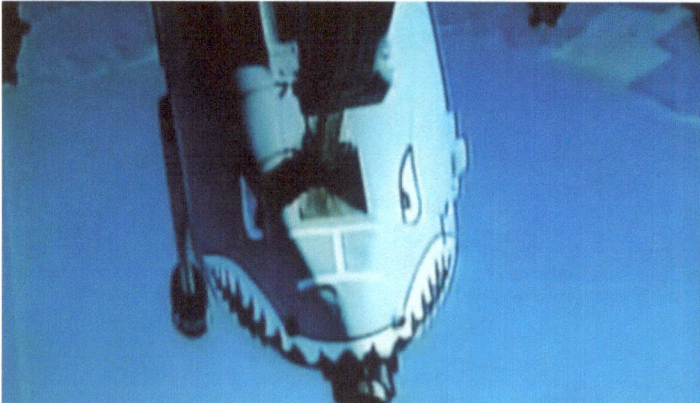

Libya liberation

Canadian Military

Alberta - Stony Plain March 9th 2011

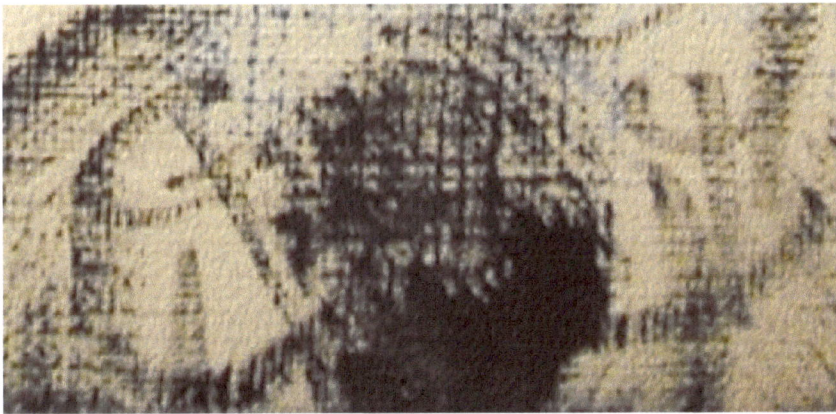

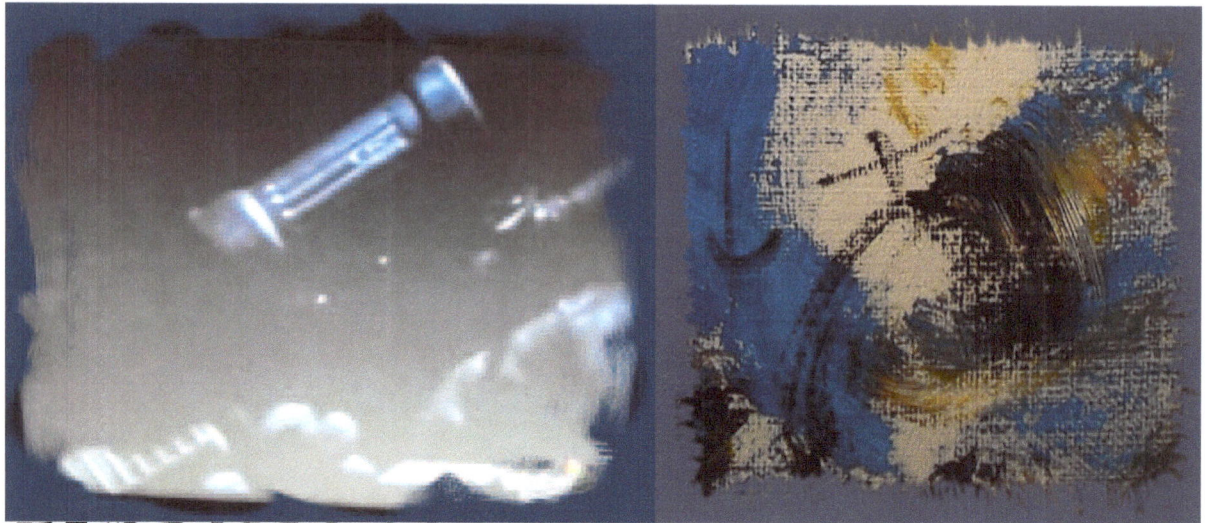

# Edmonton Garrison
## quantum psi paints just call the base for their monthly lessons in dragaon psi easy fun affordable

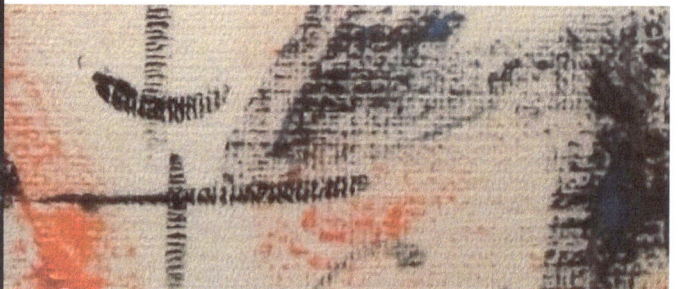

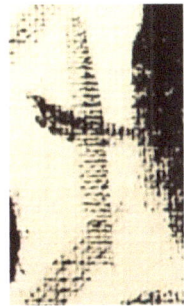

Psi paint by 1st 5th (excerpt) match to Gaddafi compound strike in Libya, by NATO forces 2011

Usama Bin Laden visual descriptive 'bin in cave' (white form, on blue background)

## USA NAVY SEALS Team 6
## Usama bin Laden - killed May 1 2011

SEALS Team 6 special ops seen from above as small black dots entering capture/kill site at  Bin's for fire fight then sending him on to Davy Jones Locker; swimming with guns

SWASHBUCKLING JOHNNY DEPP QUANTUM PSI TIME SYNCH LINKS IN REAL TIME TO REAL US NAVY SEAL - UBL kill

UBL Usama Bin Laden with tent chat visuals; psi linked to the Special Ops take down.

Psi by 1st 5th visual of Usama Bin Laden; (US) Spec Ops Col O North; note code chat dark orb white dots a visual descriptive marker in RV terminology, see Snake Eyes

Edmonton Garrison, Edmonton, Alberta, Canada
Major to Barnes, New commanding officer, 2011

1st Major as commanding officer since 1941

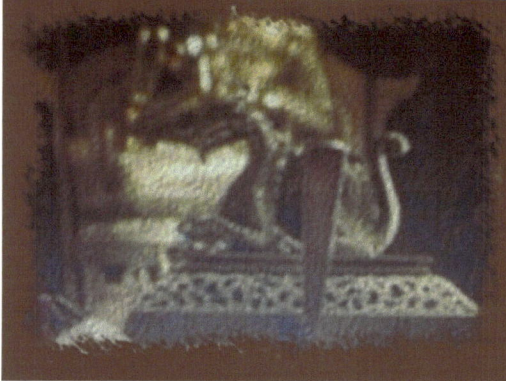

*Shanghai Knights* starring Jackie Chan & Owen Wilson; Martial Arts Sabre emote

Note: (upper right of top left photo) HOUDINI marker/see *SNAKE EYES* by 1st 5th

(below) The ancient *ORACLE* was paid great wealth by Kings and Rulers looking for the Prophecy; known for the quantum prediction of WOODEN WALLS still echoing .....

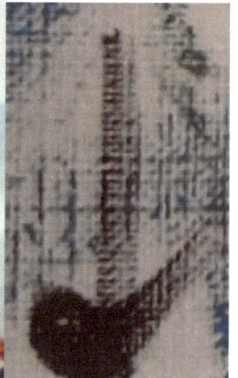

former *SEAL* Charlie Sheen, oh the humanity of it all.... We do extreme here on the Star Trail
....*rather well, actually*

www.ingramcontent.com/pod-product-compliance
Lightning Source LLC
Chambersburg PA
CBHW061054090426
42742CB00002B/37